Surfacing

Morwenna Griffiths

ISBN:: 9798374604504

For Jan

my good friend for more than half our lifetimes
who encouraged me to produce this book.
Thank you for everything.

CONTENTS

My human condition   1

Grace   3

A day out at the beach   5

This tangled life   6

Crow   8

Happiness   9

The community woodland   11

Wonder   12

On the Annapurna circuit   13

Time and being   15

A year in Edinburgh   17

October   18

Our street in November   19

Autumn wind   20

Bleak midwinter   21

Season of ice   22

Snow   23

January   24

Goodbye January   25

Weatherscape   26

Music of the shore   27

The seagull   28

Moral philosophy, logic and metaphysics   29

Trees and me   30

In the Pentlands   31

Longniddry Bents   32

Midsummer woodlands   35

Contentment   36

Plans   39

My lying camera   40

Invisible and visible   41

Beneath the surface   43

Grandmother's Footsteps   44

The wooden stool in our living room   45

Mbeya   46

Dislocation   48

On sifting through my father's photos   51

My life in lipstick   52

These hands   54

Metamorphosis   55

Time and being   56

Iridescence   58

Dreaming   59

I
My human condition

A moment of grace

It was that long, so very long journey,
stopping and starting,
the journey from Cambridge
across the flat plains of Lincolnshire,
the endless
plains of Lincolnshire.

Too tired to read,
I stared at flat lands
held by a half globe of cloudy skies
until, as I looked
at some green meadows by a winding river,
there was a white,
perfectly white horse careering,
galloping,
as though she hoped to keep time with the train,
that slow train.

A moment, and we'd left her behind,
as we jolted along towards our final stop.

Seacliff beach, East Lothian

A day out at the beach

The sun's out,
the children shout,
so −
      a lovely day.

The world turns,
the world burns,
and −
      we had a lovely day.

The air thickens,
the air sickens,
but −
      didn't we have a lovely day.

The air sickens,
the world burns,
the children shout,
so −
      did we have a lovely day?

This tangled life

I sing the wildness of weeds and their flowers,
I sing, and my face breaks into smiles,
I sing the dandelions, toadflax and buddleia.
I bathe in their colourful, scented exuberance
as they rise up from paved places,
as they erupt from brick walls,
as they lean down from roof tiles.
I sing of the courage, the resilience, of weeds.

I sing the power of insects that plague us,
I sing, my face screwed up in protest,
I sing the midges, the tsetse, the wasps.
I marvel at their otherness from me,
how their bodies lift up on transparent wings,
how they undergo metamorphoses,
how they survive the onslaught of poisons.
I sing of the courage, the resilience, of insects.

I sing our inclusion
in the retreats and advances,
in the intricate dances,
of life's evolution.

Plants on a wilded area of Bruntsfield Links, Edinburgh

Crow

A crow rises from the Links,
handsome, confident corvid,
a chip in her beak as she lands

a short step from me, a human.
I sit, eating my sandwich. We are
two beings separate from the other,

but both here in the same space,
this space, on this earth,
taking sustenance from this place

where she scavenges chips. And I,
human, scavenge, ravage, the earth,
rapacious against my will.

We're separate, but tangled together,
me, bird, chip, sandwich.
The troubled earth knits us together.

We eat, sitting in the sunshine.
I, sandwich in my hand,
content to watch the crow

sharing the sunshine, sleepily.

Happiness

There's no accountancy for happiness,
no numbers on spreadsheets,
no listing of wrongs and rights.

Happiness just comes,
or goes,
in its own good time.

A glimpse of amber leaves
against a louring sky,
a cup of fresh brewed coffee
brought in by a friend,

are blessings,
unlooked for, bestowed,
unaccountable.

Gifford Community Woodland

The community woodland

We'd cool air, tall trees, the canopy scattering sun
on emerald moss; a woodland walk, that day's delight,
though an undertow of future grief flows on.

An enchanting place – but it may soon be gone,
scorched or drowned, as politicians fight:
no cool air, tall trees, nor canopy scattering sun.

A happy day we'd had; and there are more to come,
but we're aware of our earth's climate plight.
So an undertow of future grief flows on.

The complex web of woodland's finely spun
by beetles, lichens, leaves and birds in flight:
thus, cool air, tall trees, a canopy scattering sun.

We'd fallen trunks of trees to rest upon,
while swirling clouds of insects caught the light,
and an undertow of future grief flowed on.

Has a juggernaut of venal power now won
with its self-regarding plans and blinkered sight?
An undertow of future grief flows on
through cool air, tall trees, the canopies scattering sun.

Wonder

Late in the evening, the sunset sky was filled
with the rushing, unfamiliar forms of bats
woken by the gathering dark to fly,
oblivious to us, their wondering watchers,
oblivious to our merely human seeing, mis-seeing,
understanding, mis-understanding
of their kind.

The great company swept over us,
reminding us of other ways of being,
of intricate worlds of scent, of hearing,
of welcoming the warm, dark, convivial night to come.

Reminding us of other ways of being.

On the Annapurna Circuit

Just me on the rickety wooden balcony
      of the little tea-house
            in the foothills of the Himalayas.
Behind me are the high peaks
      and the holy Machhapuchhare mountain.

Looking up from my lentils and rice
      and cup of ginger tea,
I see an eagle floating
      at eye-level,
            uninterested in me.

I am blessed by her presence.

II
Time and being

A year in Edinburgh

Autumn (The House of the Binns)

Field path. Black leaf mould,
clinging moss, golden lichen,
bronze fungus fruiting.

Winter (Cammo)

Fallen leaf, frost-rimmed.
Sleeping trees border white fields.
Breath seen on cold air.

Spring (The Western Approach Road)

Warm sun in blue sky,
roadside bushes dusted green.
Gold forsythia.

Summer (The Meadows)

Cold wind, summer rain,
ripples in roadside puddles.
Inverted branches shudder.

October

Bare branches reach up.
The highest twigs shine silver,
caught by late sunlight.

The birch leaf whirling,
glittering, golden in sunlight,
falling onto concrete.

Our silver birch tree
is dressed up in gold sequins.
She's been Strictlyfied.

Marchmont, Edinburgh

Our street in November

The wind blows whirling leaves in wild jigs.
We see each morning gutters run with gold
while roadside trees dress up as scrambled eggs.
A kind of magic on the year is scrolled –
in spite of the increasing dark and cold.

So I know, I *know,* I shouldn't be complaining.
But yes, I am. Again, it's bloody raining.

Marchmont, Edinburgh

Autumn wind

There are some leaves, I see, which smugly hold tight.
Others let go and enjoy a wild flight.
They're rolling and tumbling and scudding together.

The tree shrugs her shoulders, whatever the weather.
She shimmies and sways, holding on with her roots:
leaves come and they go. She gives not two hoots.

Bells Quarry Woodland, West Lothian

Bleak midwinter

In the bleak midwinter
with more rain on the way,
earth stands sodden, puddled,
every bloody day.

Grey on grey clouds gather,
smearing out the light.
Daytime briefly punctuates
endless winter nights.

Yet, in the bleak midwinter
on branches bare of green,
while long cold months await us,
new buds can be seen.

Ice patterns on a car bonnet

Season of ice

Streets shine yellow.
Reflections glitter
on slate-grey pavements
in this season of ice.

Wind, high and cold,
gusts round corners
and shivers down narrow stairs.

Pigeons coorie in under high girders.
Cold has seized their wings.
The long, dark night waits.

Snow

Snow is falling, drifting downwards,
Stealthy, slow, transforming streets.
Cars stand silent by the roadway
in overcoats of crystalled water.

Breugel figures soon appearing;
children running, slipping, sliding,
parents pulling bright new sledges,
people walking dogs with jackets,
grannies penguin-walking slowly,
trees above them lined with white.

Streets transformed from winter darkness
into shining winter light.

January

The sky is masked with cloud, a sheet of grey.
Black twigs of trees reach up. No sign of life.
Grass is white with frost, leaves mulched dark brown.
The world's closed down.

                                        Not quite, I'm glad to say.
It's clear to see each day brings us more light.
The year has turned. New life is on its way.

Goodbye January

I don't want to wish my life away
but I'm glad to say –
January with its skies of grey
has had its day.
Hurray!
We're on our way
to February, March, and April, May.
Yay!

Today the sky's been blue, blue, blue.
The sun's shone warm the whole day through
and the days are getting longer too.
Spring's round the corner – yes it's true!
Whoo hoo!
(And I think you think so too.)

Weatherscape

Roaring winds: the surf assaults
rocks of black in pewter seas.
Swirling, crashing water heaves
while all around the seagulls waltz.

Blustery weather, St Andrews

Music of the shore

Like moving staves of music, long waves
break white. Their tunes are made of water,
a foaming, moving scherzo. In counterpoint,
the solid, steady staves of coal-black stone;
a frail descant from our voices high above.

Cliff-top view , St Andrews

The seagull

She clasps the wall with strong webbed hands
close to the seas in Northern lands.
Ringed by the clotted clouds she stands.

She cares not for the raincloud squalls.
She watches from the ancient walls;
lets rip her raucous mocking calls.

Gull and wall, St Andrews

Moral philosophy, logic and metaphysics

At the doorways of philosophy
flowered lines of regularity
exhibit the propriety
of lives of rationality.

The philosophy department, St Andrews

Trees and me

I wish I were a cherry tree
waving its pink hair with glee.
With all the bulges round its middle,
I look quite like one, you'll agree.

Perhaps I'd be a tall grey ash.
Its bright green hair cuts quite a dash.
Again, I think its quite like me:
when limbs get jolted, down they crash.

But best to be an avocado.
(A child, I was an aficionado.)
A tree so good to perch and read in,
happily incommunicado.

Cherry Tree Walk, Edinburgh

In the Pentlands

Ripples of peat-coloured water are scattering light,
gorse scented like coconut, trees newly dressed in pale green.
Clouds drifting in lapis-blue skies are cotton-wool white.

It's April and lockdown is easing. At last we take flight,
go out of the house, leave the town, go off-line, turn off screens,
see ripples of peat-coloured water scattering light.

Nearby hills, well-known and familiar: we thought that they might
disappoint. But after a break of a year, they're as if newly seen.
Clouds drifting in lapis-blue skies are cotton-wool white.

The glimpses of hills through the woodlands fill us with delight.
Crossing the burn, we're entranced by its glitter and gleam,
its ripples of peat-coloured water scattering light.

On, up the path, distant blue moors come in sight,
far-off sheep, turf hillsides, some hikers. We drink in the scene.
Clouds drifting in lapis-blue skies are cotton-wool white.

Time for lunch. We return down the path, the gorse glowing bright,
eat sandwiches, apples, while sitting in woods by the stream.
Clouds drifting in lapis-blue skies are cotton-wool white.
Ripples of peat-coloured water are scattering light.

Longniddry Bents

Along the Firth of Forth
between the headland rocks
are strands of sloping sand.
Above the beach, low dunes,
below, a shimmering sea
under a changing sky.

Now blue, now grey, the sky
is mirrored in the Forth,
in the surface of the sea.
We walk across black rocks,
across the grassy dunes
and along the length of sand.

Yellow and coal-black sand
under a gusting sky
creates the crumbling dunes
now blowing back and forth:
remains of shells and rocks
ground down by rain and sea.

A child runs in the sea
after playing on the sand.
On waves, white seabirds rock,
then soar across the sky.
Windsurfers venture forth.
Cars cluster on the dunes.

Grey buckthorn on the dunes,
pewter, like the sea
as rain drifts down the Forth.
It glistens on the sand
beneath a glowering sky,
while water pools on rocks.

Molluscs cling to rocks,
samphire webs the dunes,
gannets hover in the sky,
then dive into the sea.
Our footprints in the sand
have washed into the Forth.

Grey-black rocks hem the sea.
Dunes are green above the sand.
A fluid sky colours the Forth.

Longniddry Bents, East Lothian

Blackford Hill, Edinburgh

Midsummer woodlands

When –
fields shimmer with heat and
air is heavy, unmoving,
as sun radiates from the sky,

Then –
Praise to the woodlands,
      peat-dark
            in their shadowed spaces.
Praise to the bracken,
      deep green,
            uncurling as it rises.
Praise to the leaf canopy,
      emerald,
            backlit by the sun.
Praise to the foxgloves
     in livery of royal purple
          for midsummer.

Contentment

Two old birds sit in mild meditation,
surveying the passing scene.
In a tree, in the shade, sits a pigeon.
Nearby, on a bench, is me.

We're both unremarkable birds.
Do you think that we care about that?
The idea that we do is absurd:
both of us happy, relaxed.

She's hunkered right down in the tree,
half asleep in her quiet contemplations,
feathers fluffed. And chilled out, just like me;
two old creatures enjoying the sun.

A pigeon, Blackford Pond, Edinburgh

Swanston, Edinburgh

Plans

Rain: fat raindrops flung against our window pane.
Not good. That day we'd planned to walk into the hills.
We'd hoped we'd go a little way beyond the lane,

and through the woods, climb steeply up until
we'd be among the gorse, raised high above the town.
Then back down the slope, to where we'd booked a meal.

Not good. Had our weather goddess let us down?
We thought maybe she had. But still, we had to go:
the meal was booked. And after all, we wouldn't drown.

Then, as we drove there, bright blue sky began to show.
Of course, she hadn't let us down! The rain had dried
– though violent gusts of wind threw branches to and fro,

and blew us about and made us laugh when we arrived.
So we took a lower path than we had planned,
but high enough to see, below, the town stretched wide.

Above, the hills stood tall; rough rocks, scrub, untamed land,
while, on our path, flowers and grasses, trees, all blew
wildly in the wind. So not at all as planned.

Instead, some new delights. Weather goddess, thank you.

My lying camera

Season of mists, and gales, and long dreich days.
Each year my lying camera tells of sun,
blue skies and back-lit leaves of shining copper,
polished brass, and gold. Mellow days.

But rain clouds lour while fallen leaves lie squelched.
A sodden, slippery mulch. Their days are done
and drizzle makes the pavement puddles shudder.

Edinburgh pavement

III
Invisible and visible

Beneath the surface

Their depths are alive.
Silent waters of the moat
circling the manor.

Grandmother's Footsteps

Behind my back, and step by step, they come.
I whirl. Time seems to stop. But, step by step,
another year, another, and another.
I see a change each time I whirl and check.
The I who once I was, I am no longer.
Surprised, bemused, I see who I've become,
but when I look, I find I've changed again.
So always, who I am, I am not yet.
Who will I be next? One answer's plain.
The old age self I'll be, I can't select.
Will I of loves and friends be dispossessed?
Be shamed as body fails or mind has gone?
Or will I live my life's last years with zest
and, contented, die still singing life's sweet song?

The Sukumaland stool

The wooden stool in our living room

Long ago a tree grew strong, tall and straight.
Its hard wood was nourished by the land,
African land, Sukumaland, Tanzania.
Tanzania, my childhood home.

The tree was felled.
A slice of the trunk was cut, carefully,
ready for a skilled and practised Msukuma
to carve, from the single piece of wood,
a low round seat, suitable for a chief
to be seated, just a handsbreadth higher than his people.

The wooden stool was presented to my Dad.
It was low seat where he used to rest,
relax, be comfortable, at ease,
in our new home
in Europe, Kent, England.
England, my teenage home.

Now the wooden stool is in my living room
in Edinburgh, Scotland.
I love the gold and black age-rings
on its polished surface.
They are like the wrinkles on my aging face,
which is smiling, as I remember my Dad.

Mbeya

I think Loleza mountain's calling me.
Though happy that colonialism's done,
my childhood's scents and sounds are still in me.

Uhuru! Tanganyika's – Tanzania's – free
and my long life is nearly run.
I think Loleza mountain's calling me.

It whispers of an avocado tree,
me climbing it: its highest branches won.
My childhood's scents and sounds are still in me.

Poinsettia bush, the back lawn for tea.
Taste of Mpishi's cheezy straws: perfection.
I think Loleza mountain's calling me.

Making pumice flakes go racing free
down furrows dug for garden irrigation.
My childhood's scents and sounds are still in me.

Always through our windows I could see
the tawny hillside, sun, a fir plantation.
I think Loleza mountain's calling me.
My childhood's scents and sounds are still in me.

Loleza mountain, Mbeya, Tanzania

Dislocation, May 2018

First full day back in Africa.
Fading light in the sudden dusk,
a pewter sky.

I find I'm bathed in a flood of familiarity:
the shadows of childhood memories,
of journeys on earth-packed roads
through miles of thorn scrub.

I follow a footpath through knee-high bushes.
Their thorns, finger-long, are soft grey
as they catch the last of the light.

Suspended from umbrella-shaped acacia trees,
the globes of weaverbird nests
form silhouettes against the glowing sky.

I know photographs will not distill
this moment,
these recollections,
this recognition of belonging here.

I also belong a continent away,
the far side of the equator,
in a rain-soaked country,
where, right now, thorn bushes are exuberant
with May blossom.

Weaverbird nests, Molepolole, Botswana

My father, Jock Griffiths

On sifting through my father's photos

Half a lifetime's buried in these slides,
my father's chosen memories unearthed
from thirty years of storage since his death.
I see us there, our many younger selves
smiling, posed, the family he loved.
I see his love of foreign places, travel:
the peaks he loved to climb, the distant hills.
This man I knew so well – but maybe not?
Forty years he'd lived before my birth.
I see in these small shards of coloured plastic
the scenes he chose to focus on and keep:
something of who he was – not just my Dad.
I also see so much of him in me,
that he's lived on for decades after death.

My life in lipstick

At five, lipstick was fun:
red, smearing my mouth, as I looked at myself in Mum's mirror,
though I shouldn't have jammed it back in its tube.

At fifteen, lipstick marked my no-longer childish face:
so pale, nearly white, contrasted with the black round my eyes.
All eyes and no mouth looked cool, or so I thought.

At twenty-five, I wore no lipstick at all.
Long hair, bare feet, one with the folk,
at least, with those folk who sang in folk clubs.

At thirty-five, I was altogether too feminist
to have any truck with make-up at all,
though I dyed my very short hair pink.

At forty-five, I applied for senior jobs which
were more normally done by men.
I was advised, correctly, to wear lipstick. I bought some.

At fifty-five, I discovered that I had become invisible: just
another aging woman. But lipstick
and black on my eyebrows, makes me reappear.

If I so choose.

Postscript:
Not my decision I know,
but what would I want the undertakers to do?
Of all my lipsticks what should they choose?

Not blood-red, I think, and surely not blue.
Ice-pink, perhaps, I wouldn't refuse
on my lips when I go.

These hands

When you look at my hands
                                 I want you
to wonder where they have been,
to look beyond the age spots and wrinkles,
to notice scars as scars of a life,
to know that these hands have been lived in.

They're a voice from earlier decades
whispering,
          vibrating,
                    reverberating,
a recording etched in the grooves of my skin,

while the whorls of my fingerprints, there from my birth,
are overwritten and smoothed as they move towards death.

Our hands

Metamorphosis

If I were a time of day,
      I would be sleepy afternoon,
            before a brisk walk.
If I were a sound,
      I would be roaring of trees in the wind,
            and the quiet surrounding it.
If I were a colour,
      I would be turquoise,
            partly blue, partly green.
If I were a place,
      I would be the edge of the sand,
            where the waves lap up and retreat.

If I were a time of day,
      I would be late morning,
            after coffee, before lunch.
If I were a texture,
      I would be smooth sandstone,
            carved and sharply incised.
If I were a shape,
      I would be a spiral,
            turning outwards, widdershins.
If I were a place,
      I would be the fringe of a woodland,
            between deep shade and full sunshine.

Time and being

I

"When you retire, what will you do?"
 Some people said to me.
"I'm not thinking what to do," I'd say,
"I simply want to be."

No deadlines hanging over me,
no lists of what I've done:
enough to see what films are on,
enjoy the summer sun.

When sitting chatting with a friend,
no need to rush and go.
"You keeping busy?" people ask.
Smiling, I say, "No!"

Craigieburn Garden, Moffat

II

And yet – the busy life I had,
that was happy too.
Focused days. Each hour was filled
with always more to do:

a book to write, a class to teach,
another marking sheet,
a conference call to organise,
a paper to complete.

I wouldn't wish all that away.
It's part of she who's me.
But now I've space for more than that.
I'm taking time to be.

Craigieburn Garden, Moffat

Iridescence

Suppose we could iridesce.
Suppose we could,
like a blanket octopus,
release ripples of shimmering
sheets of colour as we swim.

Suppose we could iridesce.
Suppose we could,
like a lizard,
flick a sudden flash
of our head and limbs.

Suppose we could iridesce.
Suppose we could,
like a butterfly,
rise on the air, glistening, until
we chose to shut our wings.

Suppose we could
inhabit other bodies, other minds,
other ways of being,
and learn to love them
as we love ourselves.

Dreaming

Dark skies cities slept,
minds danced, abandoning prose.
Dreams, stars, moon, in phase.

Blue moon, January 2018, Edinburgh

Notes

Page 13 'On the Annapurna Circuit'
Machapuchhare (Mach-a-pooch-ha-ray) is a sacred mountain in Nepal.

Page 28 'The seagull'
The poem is modelled on Tennyson's wonderful poem, 'The eagle'.

Page 30 'Trees and me'
When I was a child I lived in East Africa. In the garden there were avocado trees which I loved climbing.

Page 31 'In the Pentlands'
The Pentlands are a range of hills south of Edinburgh. The poem was written during a series of lockdowns at the time of the covid pandemic.

Page 40 'My lying camera'
This was written partly in response to Keats's famous poem, 'To Autumn', which begins, 'Season of mists and mellow fruitfulness'.

Page 44 'Grandmothers Footsteps'
Grandmothers Footsteps is a children's game we used to play.

Page 46 'Mbeya'
As a child I lived in Mbeya, a town in Tanzania, overlooked by Loleza Mountain. Tanganyika merged with Zanzibar in 1964 to become Tanzania. There were pumice flakes in the soil which I shaped into boats to float down the irrigation furrows flowing through the garden.

Page 48 'Dislocation'
We were visiting friends in Molepolole, Botswana. Their house was set back from the road with thorn scrub in between.

Page 51 'On sifting through my father's photos'
My father's photos were taken before digital cameras became available. Many of them are on transparencies.

ABOUT THE AUTHOR

Morwenna Griffiths lives in Edinburgh. She used to teach in schools and universities and has published many books and articles on education, philosophy, feminism, sustainability, and social justice. Now retired, she writes poems and takes photos instead of producing academic texts. This is her second collection of poems. The first, *Lockdown*, was written in 2020-2021, reflecting on the experience of living through the covid pandemic.

Printed in Great Britain
by Amazon

21641456R00040